A
Carnival
of Poems

and Other Curiosities

Stan Badgett

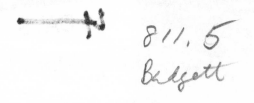

ISBN-13: 978-1499541755

Also by Stan Badgett: *Rock Dust*, Swallow's Nest 2010 and *Tenuous*, Globeflower Press 2012.

Portions of this collection first appeared in the following publications:

"A Place to Think" in New York *Quarterly*, Issue 64, 2005.

"Assumptions" in *Buckle &*, Fall/Winter 2006.

"At Cumberland Knob" in *Salamander*, Volume 18:1, Winter 2012/13.

"At the Corner of Red and Green" in *Wisconsin Review*, Volume 43:1, Fall 2008.

"Black Salt Box" in *Many Mountains Moving*, Volume 8:1, 2008.

"Coal Ridge" in *Old Red Kimono*, Volume 39, Spring 2010.

"Dutch Creek #1" in *Red Wheelbarrow*, Volume 7, 2006.

"Exit Music" in *Iodine Poetry Journal*, Fall/Winter 2005/2006.

"Human Action" in *Epicenter*, Volume 10, 2007.

"I Have Walked a Thin Path" in *Fulcrum*, Number 6, 2006.

"Inferno" in *Wisconsin Review*, Volume 43:1, Fall 2008.

"Interminable Winter" in *Dirty Goat*, Volume 17, 2007.

"I Saw the Photograph" in *Controlled Burn*, Volume 12, Winter 2006.

"Jolly Old Roger" in *RiverSedge*, Volume 24:2, Fall 2011.

"Life Is Sweet" in *Dirty Goat*, Volume 17, 2007.

"Magnificent Obsession" in *Euphony*, 2005.

"Mine Inspector's Walk to the Fan" in *Poem*, Number 94, November 2005.

"One Man Band" as "Monotonous Marching Music" in *GW Review*, 2012.

"On the Flattops" in *Meridian Anthology*, Volume 4, 2006.

"On the Scene" in *Riversedge*, Volume 22:1, Spring 2009.

"Quest" in *descant*, Volume 45, 2006.

"Rescue" in *Carquinez Poetry Review*, Volume 4:4, 2005; and *Hampden-Sydney Poetry Review*, Winter 2005.

"Said the Merchant to Simon" in *Natural Bridge*, Number 15, Spring 2006.

"The Benefits of Empire" in *Euphony*, 2005.

"There Goes Dorothy" in *Dirty Goat*, Volume 17, 2007.

"The Superintendent Brings Me a Toasted Butterfly" in *The Chaffin Journal*, 2006.

"Truro Lake" in *Mountain Gazette*, Number 105, July 2004.

CONTENTS

I

II

III

IV

V

FOREWORD

When Stan Badgett loads you onto the ferris wheel of his *Carnival of Poems*, you'd better hang on. Because, like a mischievous roustabout, he's prone to rock your car, or spin the wheel so fast your stomach lurches. But Badgett's particular gift is parking you at the apex of the ride and holding you there for a breathless moment that makes you think: "Yep. I'm gonna die. But look at that view!"

Badgett is a holy rascal, with an approach to language that careens from wry erudition to dead-on simplicity. His poetry comingles the linguistic acrobatics of Gerard Manley Hopkins, the paradoxical mysticism of William Blake, and the steel-town grit of Bruce Springsteen.

His wide-ranging intellect never gets in the way of his literal humility; he knows he's dust and to dust he shall return. But while he's here, he's gonna dig, and swing, and stare, and paint, and scribble his way through each moment as if his life depended on it. And maybe it does, for all of us.

Badgett is a man of faith plagued by doubts, a simple country boy vexed by urban angst, an erudite philosopher scalded by the coal seam that smolders in his belly. And if you listen closely, the calliope at his carnival sings like a canary in a mine shaft, each note trembling with dark mortality and humming with divine light. Badgett reminds us that even the deepest pit is, by definition, an opening. And a surefire place for the light to shine in.

—*Kristin Carlson, playwright and poet*

I

Man sets his hand to the granite rock and lays
bare the roots of the mountains.

—*Job 28:9*

ARBOR GOLD

Swish-swish
Walking in the grass
Scattered change forecast
Throughout the forest

Umbels on umbels
Withered rags
Lemon leaves
Your fingers made them

Father, I want to always
Be your friend

LIFE IS SWEET –
SWEET AS A GREENGAGE PLUM

Willows stand stickwiddled against
Specks of dashing snow

I gaze through the wavering window
The day's gotten gloomier by a shade

Snow crisscrosses, spiraling
Thunder rolls down-valley
River slides quietly by

The brightness
Amber, umber, ocher, greygold, green
Our pondworld is smiling again

COAL RIDGE

Five black dots—no, six—
    on a white hillside

Too hot for snow to stick

The seam's been burning
    for a hundred years

Blowout of the century

DUTCH CREEK #1
APRIL 15, 1981

Fifteen men
Waiting to descend
Into the hole, joking
Squinting at the sun
Having a smoke
Taking in the valley's sweep
Waiting for the trip to roll
Some wishing they were home
Staring at muddy boots
Daydreaming

The hoistman pays out the rope—
A fleeting glimpse of sun
Riding into the portal
For the last time

BLACK SALT BOX

Covered with green wooden snowflakes, stands at
  forest's edge on mine-crib stilts. Big enough
  for one hermit, snuggles family of
  six. They spit-bathe in a porcelain pan;
  draw water from the sometime-flowing ditch
  spring. For their privacy, a screen next to
  the mattress. The evening's entertainment:
  William Bradford's Of Plymouth Plantation.

Father tracked daughter out into the snow
  till her footprints stopped at a rough pine trunk.
  Living there had driven her up a tree.

INTERMINABLE WINTER

March 31   Riot of blackbirds singing their
            hearts out. Why are they so exuberant?
            A foot of snow fell two days ago,
            THUMP! and it's been gray. No green
            anywhere, but spring is gonna win,
            I know it is.

April 12   Still snowing. Socked-in for two weeks.
            This should've been our winter
            of contentment. But we've done
            all right, thanks to the Lord.

May 16   Still snowing. We're not giving up.

C SHIFT

Have you ever done time with the boys on graveyard
      with the easygoing boys, too tired to be ornery?

So weary the airpipes hiss at you
      and sleep like a seductress
            whispers to you from comfy-looking crosscuts?

When your thighs pushing uphill
      feel like plastic bags full of lactic acid
            and space and time run like LePage's
glue?

Slipping sideways, you fall down on the job
      your consciousness worn thin as paper

Then you hit the shower, and livened
      by its jet-warm spray, you go charging
         out into the day

MINE INSPECTOR'S
WALK TO THE FAN

He skates like Hermes
     on the dust, his
Bug-light clattering as it swings
     from his belt

It's a lonely walk,
     the roof collapsed in heaps
Water gurgling somewhere
     back in no-man's land

Roof's mouth open
     spilling dazzling icicles
Glass penguins scuttering
     across the floor

Dates and names chalkwritten
     on rusty arches
The wind is roaring in the
     portal

Tonight—the stars
A big black basketful of them

SAID THE MERCHANT TO SIMON

I've this dandy bucket of botulism
For you to sample. Go ahead, try a pinch
Just a pinch, it won't kill you

Hold your nose, try a spoonful
See there it's not so bad
Now swab your tongue with the stuff, and
Speak to the world. They like it

Dip your ugly stick in it
And brandish it menacingly. They'll see
You're a power with which to contend

Now don't retch. Try a belly-full
Be my empty-headed chuff
With chattering wooden jaws

Without bowels without
A soul without a brain

JONAH

Deep in the bowels, roaring clanking
Booming snapping
Coal mine

Whale's belly,
Subterranean city where they spit
On the name of the Holy One

Yet the deeps of the earth
Are in the Lord's hand

Been bumping my head on this top
A lot lately

Maybe I'm about to pop this cocoon
Maybe the whale will spit me out

INFERNO

See with what heat these
Dogs of Hell advance

Under twenty-five hundred
    feet of overburden
Dagon enters the lists

Revilings, provocations
Trumpets blasting in my ears
Red-hot hatchets flying

Gobs of spit
Layers and yet more layers of false doctrine
Doctrines of demons centuries-thick

Men boasting of their power to defile
Dancing their ritual dance
    in a commotion of tinsel and feathers

Stomping the ground
    disks clinking, placating the tio,
    the red-eyed rey Moreno of the coal mine

Their curses like ornate totems, hollow
    logs full of broken bones

The hateful names of their deities
    burning in my brain

SIGNS OF LIFE UPON EMERGING
FROM THE BLACK PIT

Dear friend,
Let me share with you what I've just seen

Butterflies in glass cases, iridescent
       sapphire wings fluttering up
           from Madagascar and Malaysia
Golden yellow butterwings, furry moths,
       pale green spoontails

Muscular black man at potter's wheel
       forming clay bowl with his fingers

God has put richness, variety
       and color into life
I love Him for that

Sincerely yours

NO MATTER

How depraved, idiotic
    rotten
God's grace is greater than them all
These unworthy thoughts
    that insist on despair shall crumble
In the palm of your persistent love

RESCUE

My favorite show is Rescue 911. None of those phony orange fireballs for me. I go for real-life TV.Junkyard Wars, the Prime Minister answering questions,Maternity Ward and shows about animals on Animal Planet.The croc hunter holding an irascible spitting cobra gingerly by the tail. Ooh, he's a big one! And the honey-colored grizzly bear who went morose and refused to eat, big booby, suffering from displacement anxiety.

But the episode that creamed my cake was this program on Animal Precinct about Sheila the tenement dog. The American Kennel Club hoists a high standard for the ideal German shepherd. She is stamped with the look of nobility, well-muscled, fearless and full of life. Her tail hangs curved like a saber. Her head is cleanly chiseled. She has dark eyes and pointed ears, she is of incorruptible character and will not bite the judge. And the coat —

The coat mustn't have hundreds of blood-sucking ticks hanging in clusters like grapes, draining the life from her anemic body. She must leap and prance, not stagger sideways, woozy-brained mutt, eyes frosted over, a tick-ridden RinTinTin. Such a mutt was Sheila. Had she a clever sense of self-parody, she would say, yours sincerely wasting away. But this is no talking dog story. Tipped off, ASPCA agents broke into the tenement yard.

Someone with phenomenal patience combed the bloated beads from Sheila's fur. Plink they dropped one by one into a surgical pan. Her supine carcass resigned to harvest hands, a tedious rescue. Recuperated, she removed from the Bronx to upstate New York, where she is prized by new owners. They say she's more than frisky, she's comical. When they brought her into the house, she ran around licking the furniture like a POW kissing the ground.

WHILE LYING
ON THE TUMMY GRASS

Geese have left white flags fluttering,
Downy white flags on gray tweed earth

Chain saw snores in fits up-valley
Children are squealing in the forest

Bless the Lord, all ye his angels
Even to improvisational music

TRURO LAKE

On my belly in a smooth soap dish
        of granite
I peer through gold gelatin
                —black slant fish

White nautilus lying still as ice
            creaks, rolls over
    cracks in two

This is the lake district
lachrymae
    bowls of aquamarine and hammered
iron

Whose steep reproach
sprinkles pink beads
    beneath our clumsy boots

In whose krasnoyarsk
  fat-bodied spiders glisten
            like pearls
  clinging to their early-warning stations

ON THE FLATTOPS

These green fields sweep away
Sweep, I say, as the sea sweeps
                    combing, brushing

A sea breeze blows across this rolling world of
            mountain grasses

Over there – at the far end of a long echo
That gash of pink and bone-white limestone

Loom-hole where her eyes rolled back
    and by the grace of God her dark eyes opened
             and she smiled

The hurtling the whirring the sliding into oblivion
Out there across the abyss it happened
When I come here I remember it

We wander, Dorene and I and the dog through tall
grass
While under our feet spelunkers crawl
    and grunt in Groaning Cave

These skunk cabbages, these wild
           geraniums and pearly everlastings!

We shall walk these windswept hills,
    walk these fields in quiet gladness

Porch on the Hill. *(photograph by author)*

II

The interrogations continued—I collected information.

—Laura Cunningham

BIRTHDAY

Interregnum of bliss—
   tales untold, yarns unspun to gold

Out into the cold red light

Pugilist fists to cling, to fight
    and not to choose,
   but make unending choices

ON THE SCENE

Three blocks from home on a summer night,
   shadows murmur under black trees,

   "Mister Miller's had a heart attack."

Across the street, Miller Motors
   is going up in flames.

An orange cauldron boils
   into the sky;

   a roof collapses, two firemen perish.

I'm seven years old, observing the world
   and its catastrophes.

END OF A BOY'S LIFE

I spent those last diminishing innocent days
        in Mrs. Dungan's attic wearing sweaters
        in lieu of heat, as they do in Britain

Joel slept on a cot by the basement furnace
We ate day-old donuts kept under the counter,
        wore laundry bags at night in the rain

With borrowed claw hammer we attacked the Bastille,
        were introduced to the subtleties of saffron

Off went my heart to Texas wrapped
        in pink paper
It came back seared and wisting of Saint Francis

Then I fell into a field of poppies. Burnt synapses
At childhood's end not Oz, but Owsley

TIEB TALK

A few times
in my life

somebody has
decked me

pasted me
in the chops

made me doe,
in tieb talk

Sometimes I
asked for it

scrawny kid
mouthing stuff

like, You more,
motman, make

me fooditz
(That's what they

did when they
made me doe:

fooditz—made
me fooditz)

QUEST

I went to this
Sensitivity session
Everyone sat in
A big circle
The guy in charge said
We're all here
Looking for answers

If anyone here
Thinks he already
Knows the answer
We don't
Want to hear it
Please keep your
Ideas to yourself

CLASS WE BRING GOOD NEWS

You are meaningless
Machines
You are accidental animals

Now
Get out there and
Fully potentiate
Yourselves

Reach
For the stars
Follow your dream

Be all that
You can be and
More besides

AN ARGUMENT BETTER
THAN PURE GENIUS

The night she is young.
Walk around, write things down. It's a big world.

He's mad, I quip back. Eyeball-to-eyeball with
Polonius.

Great scene from history: the gradual
rehabilitation of Lenin's corpse.

Hyakawa dodges chairs
thrown by bolshie radicals. His scotch-plaid
tam-o-shanter infuriates the masses.

What's driving America? High pitches
of excitement.

He offered her a cylinder of blanched,
compressed spinach. It looked like chewing tobacco.
For me? she asked.

If we continue evolving at the current rate,
we'll soon be immortal.

I SAW THE PHOTOGRAPH

It was spiderman giving interviews
To the newspaper. This was twenty-three
Years, I guess, after Shiprock. Vertigo's
Reluctant conqueror, he posed next to the
Man with an undershirt over his head.

       unicyclist
       church of world peace
       flagburner

HOW TO GET STONED

Listen,
  listen again for twenty minutes

Think of the opposite

Be a fool,
  ask the obvious question

EXIT MUSIC

It's a song we know, but can't remember
I heard angels sing it once in a dream

St. Peter's dome, like cagework opened
Giving way to celestial singing

Comely music, sweet, familiar
The tune long since goes unremembered

LINEAR B

It was tiresome to know them from the start
What exactly were they trying to prove?

Cut it how you will; damage is damage
I would like to have some consolation

ANGELUS

Delectable fat civilization
        so lovely so loud

Unlike this slender reed
        quaking in the desert

Free at Last (woodcut by author)

AT CRAGGY GARDEN

I walk through a far-fangled meadow
Past firs and hemlocks

Grass waves slightly
Fine purple grass

Hawk circles high

I take shelter under a tattered roof
From sudden fits of rain

Lean against a hand-hewn post
Sit reading Faulkner

When fresh from the drizzle
Two kids bounce in, fuzzy-

Legged boy and fine peach of a girl
She says no one likes to be tickled

He playfully answers, oh I think
They do, if they're alone

And having fun

THE CHANCELLOR

A tall woman stands in the shade
    of a crabapple tree,

attended by a photographer
    with large-format camera,

silver umbrella, and a cortege
      of photographic assistants.

As he choreographs, she leans
    against a gnarly limb.

Her black dress,
    set off by a lightweight cardigan

the color of mountain laurel,
      reminds me there is power

in simplicity.

AT CUMBERLAND KNOB

She sits on a rock navigating time,
combusting into full-fledged abstraction.

He crumples the brim of his tricorn hat.
"Come away with me to Tennessee."

He sinks at her silence. "Please talk to me."
She plucks some willow leaves, pelts him with them.

He'll face dangerous moments in the wild.
She'll grind his grits, get the gumbo boiling.

He loves her in his big casino heart,
this beautiful, blue-bonneted woman.

He's her wild turkey in the foggy mist;
she is a green canopy over him.

Their hearts cry together in the moonlight.
It's a long way to Sugarland Mountain.

FLOUNDER IN THE SEA

Soak in it
Be bold, grow old in the sea

Walk the plank. Bob belly-up
Like a soda-powered submarine

Row your
Rickety boat

Fling your flea-bitten nose
To the sea

SMOKED SWORDFISH

In a heart of palm—
The wind is invisible

What if inanimate objects
Came to life?

Harumph! Burgeoning tulips

The Dome of San Vitale
Shakes with thunder

Gold level benefits
In downtown Philadelphia

POPEYE

Marches across the page
    on his fingerknuckles

Square-jawed Don Quixote
    of the blank places,

His muscular fist
    has never had to think

On long whale-voyages
    black ships sink

Swart, swanky ships

Homage to Dissidents (collage by author)

III

Sing about the creation of all things.

—Bede

I RECOGNIZE HER
FLUTTERING TRESSES

I recognize her fluttering tresses,
                    her rusting gold
chevrolet in commuter traffic,
     bristling with arrows

     in the aspen grove
        a modern log cabin
                    bubinga basketball court

barefoot carpenters ply their calipers
     and gimlets
as relaxed as honeymooners in bora-bora

may we fire our works in your ditch?
     you may fire them on street or water.

     it cannot be rendered in gold
it remains unciphered in the blackwellian
     interplex of prescriptions
                    filled by richard estes

william conniver and haarald
     the hard-driving bargainer sailed to england
                    on opposite winds
     —thin smile of the battle-axe

                         whistling
     paroxysms of blithering fire
dance and sway, children

sulfurous melting mountain
     "them gross expanding things"

IN THE GROCERY A SLUT SINGS

in the grocery a slut sings
          nobody does it as good as you
mango and guava juice rejuvenates us
                in the withering sun
       we stuff our pittance in the slot
to secure an uninterrupted flow of television

              be still,
wind,
until chopper finishes brushing over our heads
   we scratch wax-
like drips from the fox and owl
         with our fingernails

luminous lawns and meadows
         ringed with the azure world. french
caretakers inform us les riches
        come in three layers: a, b, and c

mailed off two tax payments yesterday
it's a good feeling
le paradis n'est pas artificiel

we're assigned to the diplomat's gate
to restore an umber glow to its sun-blasted beams
and planks
   his wild roses bloom as profusely as those in the
wild

   senators are attaching secondary amendments
the serbs resisted absorption
            for five hundred years

septic truck
parks upwind and pumps into a manhole

pound says the army's vocabulary consists
of almost forty-eight words

the neighbor's blinds hang shattered
his pit bull
tried to burrow through the window
cold crisp watermelon

THERE GOES DOROTHY

there goes dorothy
  she's been at the fair too long
      she looks like a hippy

whew it's hot—doozer weekend
      mixed dried beans for a dollar
  the nonchalance of the dappled crowd

the bandstand's steady throb:
      play us another lovesong
      turn it up loud

everyone will now join in
      says the bowlegged gandy-drummer
          ta – te – ta
      the sound of two sticks clacking

they shake the caxixi
      the djembe, the clacking sticks
the shaking accelerates
          to an approximate consensus

over the delta line to be with friends,
      to gnaw on a tangy porkchop

stoker coal—lump and nut,
  company housing
hollihocks cornfields cattails
          U-pick apricots

LAST TIME I SEEN HIM

last time I seen him
was in an old black and white pennebaker

each man grab a rib
       is that all that's left
        of the whale you guys caught?

    ursua is alive, but refuses to speak

opal d'orleans
        fresh from skunk cabbage wars
folds her white arms across her knees

    we'll have no killings without a trial

beyond words, her most recent treatise
    that which can be spoken of
        is not the subject of this book

    they have steel-jacketed teeth
    they have to buy their love
    they have to buy their allegiances

  osip, sit still
       our hero the mountain man
  stomps through the village, he
devastates the countryside
      you mustn't interrupt him

what are you doing for your country?
keeping my nose out of everybody's business

I HAVE WALKED A THIN PATH

I have walked a thin path,
        skirting rebar-studded tundra

arms rubbed raw from slothful movement,
        sketched a pebble wall,
    toes swirling through bifocals

bet you can't do this sez old mister
        whites-eyes-only
in his proffered hand a smooth stone
    undoubtedly from the gizzard of a dinosaur

he doesn't think he's john wayne, he thinks
        he's the rhinoceros
"I demand to know my immediate future"
    ladies please remove your eyelids

in the soft folds of your blue mountains,
        last movement of the ninth,
    navigating a preponderance of orange barrels

        I left when they started singing
save the planet

a yacht bobbing in cultured hallways
    vader-like breathing
        apparatus
imperceptible doors weeping spontaneous oil

THE SUPERINTENDENT BRINGS ME
A TOASTED BUTTERFLY

the superintendent brings me a toasted butterfly
    with buttery speckled wings

we fill in spaces between the lines and cross them out
        forest manager gives us cold o'doul's
    reserves places at the grilled rainbow

    thanks
        for a new identity in garamond
the horse a hypothesis a parenthesis a diacritical
          breathing

notes on my painter's whites survived bleach
to read:
        dark-eyed olivia queen of navarre
squarely faces the wild chicken trainer
            the sky is falling

a celtic minstrel has tickets to moscow,
      finds ginsberg overrated,
        wrote thirty-five love poems last month

his chair disappears
      before the red-nosed clown has juggled balls
          of fire or damped
      his perspiring brow

WE DIVIDED TEN DROPS

my son and I divided
    ten drops equally off the tower,
  enduring a squall of khaki rain

work in progress—
    the mestizo's lime-green color field
        splashes on my hands and shoes

I saw you sliding down the wall
                my bruised peach

today's accomplishments:

       bought a pair of italian wool
          pants at the secondhand store
        for five bucks,
           wool hat for twenty-five cents

       painted turquoise stripes
          on the blue creek grill

       scooched up a shallow scoop
         and left my white
           handprint on its smooth whale-side

       returned a stack of korzybski
         fan zines to the library

your voice on the phone from montana
    —I stare at the screen—
  rides intact from a distant prairie

PAINTER'S NOTES: THE SONAR TOWER

Rode rough on red table,
   reading shalamov's kolyma, where spit freezes
              in mid-air

Blue incisive hue of lupine, sky pilot,
       mertensia
       —olduvai's edge

Inside a golf ball on a distant hill
       rotating orange arm

Bald-headed joel played sentimental journey
on the accordion when young, now
            builds straw houses
            photographs exploding hotels

They're playing one tune after another
on lockstep radio

Wilderness phone calls:

   I've got people coming from all over. The
      government doesn't understand about delays.

   Don't disappoint me like you did last time. OK?
      I'll set you up with some smoke.

   Do your chores. Social services is coming.

The workers are numb from the altitude, the xylene
           and lack of sleep

THE ARAPAHOE, PARDON ME

the arapahoe, pardon me ambrose bierce
  fluorescing greco-roman look,
the sanded-through-to-essential
  black-box look

tiptoeing in the wind on contingent ladders
  prehensile hand to rung, propylene
                lashings, flapping dropcloths
      things you do for a living

as I slurped a furry mouthful
      of orange juice a bee
  slipped the needle into my tongue

the same gulls chortle near our house which
      chortled
          on fair mount sopris
where we curled, listening

to your faith add virtue, knowledge,
                self-control
      so two brothers urged my flaccid will
      up a red wall on a golden day

UTTERANCE: THE QUANTITY OF SPEECH

utterance: the quantity of speech put forth by one person,
        preceded and followed by silence

the interconnected web of life wears fresh paint—
        a gold and fuchsia sky

hand over heart for Old Glory, mint-flavored taffy kisses
    her cheek bears a soft comet

the flag defiant on his t-shirt
            "just try and burn this one"

the air turns faintly yellow; windshields burn dull orange
            the woman with copiously tattooed forearms says
        have a cool one on me

            black trees sway before an orchid inkblot sky
distant ash settles
    fists of smoke plunge heavenward

EXCITEMENT CITY

So horny babe can't hardly think
Look
Rex the wonder horse in bulging leotards
        thrusts his slobbering mouth onto the
        microphone, sings baby compay

To axe-wielding valkyries
        at the gate say yes (you can't say no)
Yield to truncheon's song
Say yes to oroborical worm

Now tonight—(waits for applause
        and laughter to die down)
Tonight we're going to make love all night long

Oh city you're big
You sweat and your eyes bulge

Oh city, you're big

JOLLY OLD ROGER

I'm a big boaster, baby
Listen to me boast

Never done no wrong to nobody
Sure as I'm alive

I'm a sweet-singing magpie
Listen to me sing

I'm as harmless as they come, babe
Ain't giving you no jive

Pure cream of the crop, babe
Sweet as any man

I'm a straight-shooting huckster
Shooting straight for your hive

AT THE CORNER
OF RED AND GREEN

Echo of stars

Snowy peppers,
frosted comets—

Can you bear this
cascade of blue?

O where do you
come from

You little flakes
of snow?

Joyce in hand, I
trace Ms Steinem's

Steps into the
bright gazebo.

GENERATION THAT DOES IT IN THE DARK

There is a generation of consummate
      sophistication
That fully understands the mechanics
      of copulation
That does it in the dark and in the streets
That does it with frequency and knows
      all the positions

There is a generation
      with eyeteeth sharp as knives
For tearing to bits its offspring

JEZEBEL'S GAMBIT DECLINED

I can't get into your squirrely action
You're always promising satisfaction

You lure me with your warm embrace
Then shove a cowpie in my face

ONE-MAN BAND

A ring of mudflies
      congeals around Friar Fat
His armipotent high-gloss hair hangs, trembles
      and writhes

His yakking gums fracture the
      fragmosis
He sings is this burning
      an eternal flame?

Monotonous marching music
      out of his pelvis
      endlessly rocking

Slow it to a dog-whoofing cough syrup
Adam,
The silver dragon's wrapped round your ear

ALL DAY LASTING

When I come away from times with you
Indelible peace, as if you dipped me
In some new ingredient
Your Spirit is sweet
And it's so rare to be your candle

You will use whom you will
Even the incongruous

Bolts and Cables (photograph by author)

IV

Sometimes I share my bread and jam with yellow jackets.

—Opal Whitely

COCK OF THE WALK

Civilization's malcontento—financial mastermind—
takes from the rich and gives to the poor, prints fiat
money,
promises communes to his soldiers.

General Villa—man on horseback—dashes in, dashes
out.
Liberationist. Trickster. Grimy with dust, sipping
tequila in the sun.
First revolutionary in a century of turmoil.
Mexican pop star.

Centauro of Chihuahua—dragon in his dusty world—
he hogs more than his quarter-hour, pushes like Peary
to be famous.
Gallops north to Columbus with his golden horde,
the lions of San Pablo.

AT ROSARIO CEMETERY

Thousands of white headstones, primly ranked, radiate in all directions. A redhead sits on the curb of this marble orchard, glasses jauntily pushed back. She speaks about Manderfields entombed in the brownstone mausoleum—stained glass smashed by vandals— aloof beyond a stone wall, somehow the center of all this ordered history.

"My brother's the spitting image of William Manderfield who started the Santa Fe New Mexican. His wife Josefa was eleven years old when Kearney trotted in to commandeer the city. She had three children out of wedlock before marrying Manderfield. The Luna Mansion—that's where they brought me home as a baby." (Some Spaniards have copper-colored hair.) "Solomon Luna, active in politics, drowned in a vat of sheep dip, at least that's what they say. Josefa's daughter Pepe, my great grandmother, taught me to eat sugar sandwiches."

From the curbstone Rosario Cemetery unfurls toward the points of the compass. A sculpted horse gallops through a platter of plenty heaped on the bronze backs of an ass, pig, bull, and sheep. New Mexico holds its own among various states of contentment. The eye, lamp of the body, feasts on its freestyle sunsets, peach-patched adobes, shade-dappled armadas, roses, and tiger lilies. From this city of stone, walls extend outward, slathered with peanut butter.

An innocent wren dips its beak in the quiet fountain at Saint Francis Cathedral—the one Jean Lamy built (Willa Cather's arch-bishop)—with Yahweh's name inscribed over the bronze doors. The peace of the Lord be with you all. This same bishop sealed Jose-fa and her journalist husband, Citizen Kane of his desert empire, whence came this unassuming lady fingering a strand of Celtic hair, seated among three thousand marble tombstones, telling of sheep and cattle rustlers, scouts and congressmen, unearthing family stories, keeping the past.

THE BENEFITS OF EMPIRE

The queen's nose, recently replaced
looks down on dew-green sponge cake
freshly sliced and topped with firecrackers;
extensible calibrated rods, paper quadrants
scotch-taped autocarpus
entrails of the common worm, italian
and spanish bees in a cabinet drawer

Let us contemplate the benefits of empire
the power to memorialize
what would have been forgotten
to hoist up granite obelisks and paint
statues our national color, to think
favorably of ourselves in comparison
with other empires, and so on

Ashurbanipal II with stylized bicep,
knee and ankle; his titles
his earthly conquests
and the extent of his realm
mixed meats on marble
specimen tables, busts and pedestals

Antinus, favorite of hadrian, deified
as bacchus; mrs john ashton of liver-
pool in carved mahogany
a beam of light, a line of inquiry
culminating in cheap wallpaper

IMAGINATION

like obscenity
leafs out,
flattening the
diaphragm.

Limited in
that it cannot
acknowledge
limitation,

it flies like a
flaming couch
to the rescue.

Though
the pole sinks
deep,

in this world
there are no
bottomless
pools.

A PLACE TO THINK

Rusting vortex
You, like me, are waiting

May I follow you around
and record your comments

Oops I think
we lost something

Icarus colliding
with concrete

Yep that's what they did
—did to the color white

I rest my case
Which case is that

HUMAN ACTION

we cultivate
wonderlemons

decorate
fans, pedestals,
wine cups, boxes

build
bridges over
the Ohio

blank rectangles
powered by thought

we worship our
own ideas

make meaning
from scratch

MAN

In temporary
  suspension

Secret
    precipitate

Passes
    with ease

Through a
  sieve

Of
Preconceptions

GATHER FORMULAE INTO
PAMPHLETS

Be stubborn to the end
Let Bearcat bark his old top off
Hide in the bathroom till he passes out

Organize "Down with Illiteracy" groups
Ascribe war to all things war-like:
    earth, mirrors, anguish

PEACE PARTY

As sure as my name is Kreskin
Flash bang
Everybody's having a great time

Nonstop explosions
Pandemonium on the streets
Do we kiss?

Don't be surprised
If there are UFO sightings

IN OUR MERRY
SPACEMOBILE

Stick men are busy
   at billiards

Babies arrive
   by escalator

A foam ball floats
   into the sun

MAGNIFICENT OBSESSION

Starring the baldheaded cowboy who would walk
       a mile in his boots or kill
       for a Coca-Cola

Yes, poetry will do that all right
It will surely save the world

No, little boy, this is not a lotus
       I'm eating. It's an artichoke

ASSUMPTIONS

We think we know
whose woods these are

where the tool stops
and self begins

by whose wisdom
the hawk takes flight

who bound the cords
of sweet pleiades

whose foot treads on
the jackal—
black Anubis

SLOW DANCE

The man with long legs and no knees
nods his head like he knows what he's doing,
each thought erasing its predecessor.

A legendary twinkle in his eye
survives the invisibility test.

KILAUEA

She's talking today
       What's she saying?

She says good thing you got
       your guardian angel

River of fire eating
       decency for breakfast

She burps, and a galaxy
       of stars goes on pilgrimage
       to Elvis' grave

THE TROMPE L'OEIL ARTIST

Deft, deceptive strokes

Hair's breadth of pressure,
        fine-tip brush

Line by line the oak
        footprint disappears

A cardboard palette
        in his hand, he ponders

If my bloody feet had slipped,
        no sons or daughters

GOOD TIMES ROLLIN'

we believe yes
    but only for a little while

the royalty of rock
    the brass-wrapped bee sting

the indigo-lined
    curve of his guitar

his forehead glows
    under manufactured lights

yes yes yes
    what is it we believe?

the long hoot of pleasure

flashola zazzola
    it goes down smooth like cream

THE PARADE OF LIFE

just went hoot-tooting past my street

We're hung out to dry—all dehydrated

Aimee McPherson wore a soft halo
Mom kept a pair of angel wings in the closet

So that's where the orange curtain was, right? I recall the wind made
quick work of it

Nemo squinted through his binoculars
Natalie Wood sobbed in the dark water

A wide-ranging storm finally expires. Kids cry
in the pup tent of solitude

Alphas—they're all extraordinary
Petroleum Vesuvius Nasby
Nebuchadnezzar, the grass-eating king

Oh, yeah, that was Milo scratching his head, shuffling
down the street mumbling to himself, spaceships
drifting in over the Flatirons

Bix's inflectional syncopation
Rothko, intoxicated with drybrush

Get somebody from linguistics in here—the problem with monkeys on
typewriters. We're getting baked
in the oven of time

LORD I THANK YOU

For the easy way that
       poems sometimes come
And for the what's
       next sordid stacks

         relics

Heaps defying single bounds
       that flying overhead
       translate themselves
By your touch
At long last into poetry

Pure Honey (photograph by author)

V

And I knew the pitfalls of self-satisfaction.

——*George Kennan*

CLOSE SCRAPES WITH GREASE

Slim Perkins was the new boy on the crew, hadn't been underground long—so skinny he knocked around loose in his coveralls. Partway through the shift his caplight began to fade. One of the guys told him, "Yer old lady must be running around on ya." That's a superstition in the coal mine.

His boss looked at the fading bulb and said, "You better head out to the track and wait for another light." So Slim walked out to the track in a flickering orange glow and sat till his battery went completely dead. The tunnel turned thick black. He imagined he was floating in space, that the mine was a bottomless pit, that he was lost in outer darkness. He waited a long time.

Finally he could hear the trip rumbling further up the slope. It took forever for the rope rider to lumber down to the spot where Slim sat waiting in the dark. The rope rider handed him a fresh light, which he clipped onto the front of his hard hat. He nodded his head up and down, watching the fresh beam light up the decrepit coal seam as the car rumbled on down into the abyss.

Before he got back to his workplace, a gaggle of lights was already bobbing toward him. It was the end of the shift. When the crew reached the track, they hung back a little, eyeing him furtively. He knew what they were after. Just that day one of them had said, "You ain't been greased yet." That was Bugas.

Just the other day, by accident, Slim had swung around and clobbered Bugas in the head with a timber. Was Bugas still mad? Slim sat on a giant metal toolbox by the track and waited for the trip car to come back up from the bottom. The boss was palavering with the mine mechanic about having some drinks at the Black Nugget.

Slim looked up and noticed Bugas edging toward him, with red-haired Kid Mango slinking close behind. They bolted for him, and he instinctively jumped onto the track, where the rope rider's cable stretched out tight along the ground. Just like that the two miners were all over him, grappling his arms and feet. Bugas wrapped his big arms tight around Slim's ankles, while Kid Mango locked onto his shoulders and pulled with all his might. Another miner jumped in and latched on like he was dogging a steer.

Slim was quick and slippery and proud of it. He spun around like greased lightning, determined to break their hold, twisting round and round till finally he broke free of their grasp. It surprised them for a second—they figured they had him in the bag. He backed a little ways down the track slope, smiling under his breath. Just then the cable leaped up, and everybody jumped out of the way. The rope rider, a gray-bearded old codger named Stumpy, was coming up from the bottom. Was Slim ever glad to see him. As the crew headed out the hole, Bugas looked at Slim sideways. "We'll get you another time."

It's Friday. The trip hits daylight. The crew surges into the lamphouse. They slam their lights into the charger, rush to the time clock, and punch out. They cram through the door of the waiting bus. Slim isn't taking any chances—he's sitting close to the front. The goons are after him. They plan to finish him off. He's readied himself for this occasion as best he can. He's cinched his leather belt down two extra notches. His knife is open in his pocket. If they go after him, he's going to puncture somebody.

Radar the grim-faced bus driver manhandles the bus down the steep mountain road. He won't be any help. Slim searches the rear-view mirror and sees Bugas, then the whole busload of mangy-haired miners staring at him with contempt.

There's Crusher, living legend. One time when the boss was chewing him out he got tired of hearing it, so he picked up the boss and hung him on a post by a nail and just left him there squawking. Everybody knows that story.

Sooty looks like Bill Sykes with that jaunty long rag tied around his neck. There's bony-fingered Vermou—how he regaled them today with sadistic episodes from a recent porn flick. The floor is awash in rock dust, tobacco spit and filthy rags.

Slim stares straight ahead, minding his own business. Then a big hand clamps down on his shoulder, and a surly voice informs him, "Somebody wants you." In a snap they're all over him, yanking him out of his seat and dragging him to the floor. Sooty gets in the way of Slim's rambunctious feet and goes for a ride straight up in the air. That brings them rooting with double fury like a pack of wild pigs. There's a dozen of them on him, and in no time he's pinned to the floor, no chance to get at his knife. He's glad he cinched down his belt. They're having a heck of a time with it. He keeps pushing his stomach hard against it.

Finally they manage to unzip his fly and pump their tube of greenish-purple grease into his crotch. How would he explain this to his wife? Vermou stands over him like the Colossus of Rhodes, beady eyes alive with glory. Slim pushes impotently against their weight. He had hoped to put up a more spectacular fight. Guess that's supposed to be the lesson. The gang masters all.

Years went by and nobody tried to grease Slim Perkins. Then one day old Butch Semanski got a wild hair up his nose and started looking for a way to get him. Butch was a moose-jawed, bow-legged, barrel-chested, two-fisted section foreman with a continual look of low-burning orneriness in his eyes. Slim somehow had gotten on Butch's bad side, and Butch commenced to ride him every chance he got. What's worse, Butch incited his crew against him, so that every time he walked into Butch's section, he had to look both ways.

"Where ya going there, Perkins?" It was Butch, standing in the entry to his section.

"I have to check the face."

"Go into our section and there'll be a surprise waiting for you on your way out."

Slim headed resolutely into the section. The air was alive with mischief as he walked past the miner (a giant machine that ripped the glittering black coal out of the mountain). Some of the crew gave him knowing looks. There was a five-gallon can of Meropa sitting on the mining machine. One guy thumped it and nodded Slim's direction.

"Lord, please help me," he found himself praying as he walked down to the face. Slim loved the smell of fresh-cut coal—black and warm and sweet. He sounded the top and checked for gas. His anemometer swung up and down, back and forth across the face of coal. "Please send two strong angels to get me out of here without getting greased."

Slim headed back up the slope toward the crew. As he came around the corner, there were suddenly two bosses standing there, right beside the miner. Hallelujah! Where had they come from? A belly-full of joy crept up to his ears. It was all he could do to keep from smiling. He walked right past that can of Meropa and out of the section.

Old Badger (photograph by Hank Gray)

NOTHING FAILS TO AMAZE ME

CHARACTERS

NARRATOR	PANCHO VILLA
CEDRIC	BALTHAZAR
ATTENDANTS	SCHOLARS
CHORUS	BRASS BAND

SETTING

(A rundown coffee shop. Downtown, any city. Beat-up wooden table and two wooden chairs center stage. Two mugs of coffee. Chess board. Candle in a wine bottle on the table. Shelf full of tattered books. In the background on a counter, an espresso machine. CEDRIC and BALTHAZAR seated at table, facing each other.)

ACT 1, SCENE 1

NARRATOR: All hands on deck. The show is about to start.

CEDRIC: This will be a grim discussion.

BALTHAZAR: I know, and I'm ready for it.

CEDRIC: Get ready to sweat.

BALTHAZAR: I'm ready. What are we discussing?

CEDRIC: Truth.

BALTHAZAR: Come on. Everybody's always discussing that.

CEDRIC: There you go again, making those broad, sweeping generalizations like you always do.

BALTHAZAR:	On a lighter note, guess who stopped smoking this afternoon?
CEDRIC:	I'm a dead dog, and dead dogs don't come back to life.
BALTHAZAR:	Nothing ever happens.
CEDRIC:	The poltergeists are active this afternoon.
BALTHAZAR:	I'm a meaningless machine. Want to make something of it?
CEDRIC:	What's it all about?
BALTHAZAR:	Keep talking, stranger.
CEDRIC:	I've been talking strange all my life.
BALTHAZAR:	How long is that?
CEDRIC:	Memories are frightful things.
BALTHAZAR:	You don't have to remember all that much. How long have you been alive?
CEDRIC:	This conversation is going nowhere. I can tell that.
BALTHAZAR:	Roll on, you rolling recollections.
CEDRIC:	I remember the time.
BALTHAZAR:	Yes, wasn't those the days?
CEDRIC:	Nobody knows the trouble.
BALTHAZAR:	You can say that again.
CEDRIC:	How're we doing for progress?
BALTHAZAR:	About halfway through.

CEDRIC:	Should we take a break?
BALTHAZAR:	I feel so—interchangeable.
CEDRIC:	There's got to be some significance here, somehow.
BALTHAZAR:	There is, but I'm standing by my opinions.
CEDRIC:	I can't say it.
BALTHAZAR:	I know. It's hard.
CEDRIC:	That was the dramatic moment as far as I can tell.
BALTHAZAR:	It all goes by so fast.
CEDRIC:	So, how's your coffee?
BALTHAZAR:	Semi-sweet with half and half.
CEDRIC:	If I yell loud right here, will it make a difference?
BALTHAZAR:	Only if you pay attention.
CEDRIC:	Many voices sing over many waters.
BALTHAZAR:	Sing like a dog in the nighttime.
CEDRIC:	I'm having a grim recollection.
BALTHAZAR:	Control it. We're almost home.
CEDRIC:	Are there any obligatory scenes?
BALTHAZAR:	None we can't skip. (Clears his throat.)
CEDRIC:	Did we get to the part about "seekers for truth getting exhausted"?

BALTHAZAR:	Waiter, more coffee, please. (Lights a cigarette.)
CEDRIC:	You can't hardly tell at this stage.
BALTHAZAR:	Departmentalization has taken over.
CEDRIC:	Look out! Flying fish!
BALTHAZAR:	Man, oh man. What a life.
CEDRIC:	I think we've just gone beyond the limit.

(CEDRIC and BALTHAZAR push their chairs back and step away from the table. Each goes to a different side of the stage, where ATTENDANTS wait with towels, buckets, and spray bottles. ATTENDANTS ruffle their hair with towels, spray their faces with a refreshing mist of water, give them water to drink, pat them on their backs, hold up buckets for them to spit in. CEDRIC and BALTHAZAR return to their seats.)

ACT 1, SCENE 2

CEDRIC:	Did I miss anything major?
BALTHAZAR:	Just your life, that's all.
WAITER:	(Enters from stage right and pours BALTHAZAR a cup of coffee.)
CEDRIC:	Shall we start or shall we resume?
BALTHAZAR:	Shall we waltz?
CEDRIC:	We're always so busy. We don't have time for conversations like this.
BALTHAZAR:	Out of the heart.
CEDRIC:	Put her there, man.

BALTHAZAR:	I'm going to write me a tone pome.
CEDRIC:	Don't leave anything out.
BALTHAZAR:	Gonna grab that bull by the horns. Take that language and make it new.
CEDRIC:	We're on a roll now.
BALTHAZAR:	I believe we are moving into an amphitheater of culture.
CEDRIC:	And leaving our troubles behind.
BALTHAZAR:	You said it.
CEDRIC:	I feel a poem coming on. How's this? Cranes on the skyline.
BALTHAZAR:	That's what I meant.
CEDRIC:	Can you, can I, can any of us?
BALTHAZAR:	Spit it out. Don't mince with words.
CEDRIC:	Now for the big subjects. Sex, death, and old age.
BALTHAZAR:	I've only got one pair of teeth and they're fading fast.
CEDRIC:	I gotta grab a bite, brush my teeth, and go to the bathroom.
BALTHAZAR:	There'll be time enough for that when the dealing's done.
CEDRIC:	This is quite the conversation and has been.

(Curtain)

ACT 2, SCENE 1

(CEDRIC sits alone at table for three minutes. Silence. Tokes on a cigarette once or twice. Sips coffee once or twice.)

NARRATOR (after three minutes of silence): Here we introduce some excitement.
(Colored lights flash on and off for ten seconds. Followed by two more minutes of silence.)

(Curtain.)

ACT 2, SCENE 2

(Same setting as Act 1, but now CEDRIC and BALTHAZAR are sitting in chairs suspended two feet above the floor by wires.)

CEDRIC:	Let's have a conversation.
BALTHAZAR:	Okay. Do we have to?
CEDRIC:	Let us make something of ourselves.
BALTHAZAR:	Great wooly mammoths of history.
CEDRIC:	(Stands up, dramatically.) Attila the Hun enters his bedchamber, keels over.
BALTHAZAR:	(Eyes burning, smites his chest with clutched fist.) I, Pancho Villa, killing prisoners, taking names.
CEDRIC:	What in the heck are we talking about?
BALTHAZAR:	What do you mean heck?

CEDRIC: I think we can at least demonstrate by this drama that the workers are destined to take the reins of power and rectify the world.

BALTHAZAR: That's already been proved by history.

(Curtain)

ACT 3

(In which the significance of this play is discussed by a panel of SCHOLARS. They are shaven bald and wear dark suits.)

SCHOLAR 1:   This is definitely one of those plays that should not be performed or even read aloud.

SCHOLAR 2:   Monolithic hegemony posits the consistorial interpretative maximus distributively oppositional within constrained yet differentially super-autonomous structures manifestly legitimizing occlusive functions associatively subverting the quantitative and instrumental relations of egalitarian society.

SCHOLAR 3:   (Not to be outdone.) I have nothing to say.

(Opera music)

SCHOLAR 1: The next act isn't really about Pancho Villa.

SCHOLAR 2: Let's all shuffle off to Buffalo.

(Curtain)

ACT 4

CHORUS: Good old Pancho Villa
            Wide-eyed Pancho Villa
            Doe-eyed Pancho Villa
            Of the lowlands

(PANCHO himself enters from side, takes center stage. He cuts a dashing figure, clothed in white peasant's trousers and loose blouse of bleached muslin, sports an ample black mustache. He clenches a buccaneer's knife in his teeth and freezes momentarily into a Kabuki-like martial pose.)

PANCHO: Being a bandito is serious business. So first I begin
            by munching a Cheeto.

CHORUS: (Hums in harmony while he opens a bag of Cheetos
            and munches. Coyotes yip and yap in the distance.)

PANCHO: Oh I'm mean and rough
            And dirty and tough
            Adrift on a dark
            Sunburnt landscape

            I'm killing prisoners
            And taking names
            Far from the sheltering
            Consensus

            I'm a grizzled statistic
            A curled-up tamale
            Baked in the corn-husking heat

CHORUS: Where on earth's green planet
            Can a magpie find its wings?
            Yet I hear the voice of Pancho Villa
            Singing like a dead dog in the desert

PANCHO: (Strums on a ukulele.)
            On the bounds of one and zero
             Tom fool cat upon a fence
            Here I sing my crazy love song
            Between the airy and the dense

CHORUS: He sings to his cross-eyed lover
            Sweats it out on the blue guitar
            Yearns across an ancient boundary
            Beneath the artificial stars

(Brightly-colored papier maché stars, illuminated from the inside, are lowered from the proscenium. Sons of the Pioneers hum in the background. Coyotes start yapping again. BRASS BAND consisting of tuba, clarinet, flugelhorn, and glockenspiel strikes up a lively rendition of "Buckle Down, Winsocki" while PANCHO sings.)

PANCHO: Go, go coyotes. Go, go!
                 Win this game tonight.
                 Buckle down and fight,
                 Hit that line with all your might.

CHORUS: Oh Pancho Villa
                 He's our swashbuckling hero
                 Hot and wild hero
                 He's our salsa of the month

(PANCHO demonstrates a yearning for the land across the border by clasping both hands to his breast and gesticulating offstage.)

PANCHO: I'm packing my saddlebags
                 At midnight
                 I'm fixing to leave this place.
                 (Lays down and dies.)

CHORUS: The more he's dead
                 The more he stays the same

PANCHO: I'm a slow-moving cartoon
                 Tamale-pie frontiersman
                 Savoring my hot sauce
                 On the far side of the flat dusty river

(Curtain)

FOREARMS
by Stan Badgett

We moved to Thornton in 1960. Up the street from our house was a dinky shopping center which sported a Woolworth's, pool hall, barber shop, drugstore, and grocery. The drugstore had a U-shaped counter in the back where you could order up a cherry phosphate for a nickel. Two telephone booths stood against the wall where somebody was always chewing the fat with a boyfriend or girlfriend.

I was trying hard to grow muscles, since I only weighed eighty-five pounds. My buddy Steve Grow had a barbell in his basement with which we strove to press our own weight. Eventually I built my own barbell at home with a section of pipe and some bricks. I wanted meaty forearms like Dad's. When we sparred, he could knock me halfway across the room with a playful cuff. Comic books featured Charlie Atlas ads promising big rewards if I would learn a body-building technique called "dynamic tension." Bikini babes would cling to my biceps; bullies would keep their distance. I weighed five pounds less than the ninety-pound weakling who kept getting sand kicked in his face.

Steve and I shared a crush on Kathy, an exquisite beauty in our eighth-grade class. Slender and fine-featured, she resembled the French actress Yvette Mimieux. Steve and I spent a great deal of time poring over our attraction to her. Poor Kathy. To be the object of my perpetual gaze must have been hard to endure. I asked her out once, but she politely declined. I printed a medallion at a booth in the park—a lucky charm engraved with a four-leaf clover and a leprechaun. I stamped the letters AEIOU on one side and KATHY I LOVE YOU on the other. Danny Skole sat behind me in English class. One night I told him, "You've got to help me place this charm in Kathy's hands." He said, "Sure." We planned it so that I'd stare at my little medallion, then Danny would pester me to see it. I'd re-fuse, then we'd tussle over it. He'd grab it from me and race across the room and give it to Kathy. Then I'd come unhinged and tear into him, and we'd slug it out in the back of the room. Our opportunity came the next day. You couldn't ask for a better actor than Danny. Our performance came off perfectly, and no one realized it was a sham. The best part came when we tore into each other, aban-doning ourselves to the fury and ecstasy of the moment, forgetting about play-acting. The English teacher rushed to the back of the room to break it up. We electrified the whole class. We wowed 'em.

Kathy didn't need this kind of attention, but she managed it gracefully. She issued a brief statement. "I wish it was Eddie." (Some high school guy she liked.)

One morning I went to my locker to get my books for first-hour class and PLAM! my buddy Steve punched me in the mouth. I felt no pain, just a black squishing sensation in my face. "That's for what you called my mother," he said. At his home that afternoon, Steve's dad informed me that a neighbor had overheard me calling his wife a terrible name. Exactly what the word was no one would say. "You know perfectly well what this is about." The accusation remained maddeningly unclear. Finally he drove me home. I got out of the car humiliated and confused. I've never figured out what word it was that I supposedly said.

A new kid appeared in our eighth-grade class, handsome with wavy, dark hair. That was Chip, nephew of heavyweight boxer Gene Fulmer. The classroom fluttered with female energy when he arrived. One day I arm-wrestled him and was actually beating him. I felt cool about that—here's this guy whose uncle's a boxing champ. Then some girls noticed what was going on, and it looked like they were going to make a big deal out of it, so I dropped my arm and let him beat me.

That summer I got into a fight at the shopping center. My pal Danny and I wandered into the drugstore one evening, sidled up to the soda fountain, and ordered cherry phosphates. Three toughs sauntered in. "You're sitting on our stools," they informed us.

"Sorry," I said, "you'll have to find some other place to sit."

It warmed their hearts to find somebody who was game for a mix-up. "Let's go out back and settle this right now." That was John Cammack speaking. Lean and raw-boned, he was well-respected around school for his fighting prowess.

"OK," I said coolly. I looked at him with level eyes and uttered a really inane line. "I hope you've had your Charlie Atlas lessons."

John replied, "You'd better hope you've had yours."

We retreated to the back of the shopping center, which was dark and vacant. No Danny to be found; he had disappeared into thin air. It was just me and John Cammack and his buddies. In the glower of distant street lights John and I squared off, and in another instant we rushed each other with fists flying. Several quick jabs stung my face. I kept ducking and dancing around the way Dad had taught me to do. John's blows were glancing off me and not connecting full-force. I counterattacked, shooting for his stomach and head. In the welter of spring-loaded punches and leaping feet, exhilaration began to rise in me. I was delivering a respectable

84

performance. It surprised me. I could tell John was surprised too.

Then a bicycle whizzed by, and the kid yelled "Hey!" as loud as he could. I turned toward the bike, and at that moment John's fist slammed into my stomach. I crumpled to the ground. They helped me to my feet and asked me if I wanted to fight some more, but my will had been plundered by Cammack's grand-slam punch. There were no hard feelings. After that we treated each other with respect.

So Long (woodcut by author)

CPSIA information can be obtained at www.ICGtesting.com
Printed in the USA
LVOW07s1546290115

424893LV00003B/556/P

Made in the USA
Middletown, DE
28 June 2017